Seasonal Musings

Karen Baster

Presentation by *BookLeaf Publishing*

Web: www.bookleafpub.com

E-mail: info@bookleafpub.com

ISBN: 9789357690188

First edition 2022

The Creek

Do you remember going to the creek?
The water so still
That the reflection was a mirror.
If you took a photo, no one could tell
Which way was up,
Which was the reflection.

Do you remember going to the creek?
The lizards on the branch
Lazing in the sun.
If you made a noise, they didn't care
An opened eye, or
A twitch of their tail.

Do you remember going to the creek?
Trying to spot the turtles,
In the muddy water.
Watching for the head bobbing
Up for a breath
And disappearing.

Do you remember going to the creek?
The heron perched on the log
Preening itself.
It raised its head if you spoke,

But otherwise
Continued grooming.

Do you remember going to the creek?
The fishing lines, and rubbish
Littering the shore.
We'd take a plastic bag
And the rubbish
Leaving the rest clear.

Do you remember going to the creek?
Watching nature
Live, and be alive
When we would stop and take note,
Know each bird
And each lizard.

Do you remember going to the creek?
Exclaiming with delight
Each animal seen.
With each photo taken,
A memory preserved
For a lifetime.

The Raindrop

There's a raindrop on the window pane,
It hesitates and then stops.
Another spot falls from the rain,
It meets together, then drops.

Like spiderwebs, on the window pane,
the patterns start to form.
Each raindrop dripping leaves a stain
That's falling from the storm.

It zigs and zags down the window pane,
It takes a winding route.
A drip, a drop it starts to gain,
It echoes, 'til it's mute.

There's shaking on the window pane,
The thunder claps so loud.
The rain goes streaming down the drain,
Yet, still falls from the cloud.

A blinding flash on the window pane,
The lightning strikes so fast.
Bright and bang, thunder and rain,
It surprises with a blast.

There's a rain drop on the window pane,
It stalls a bit, then drops.
It joins another drip of rain,
The storm, it seems, has stopped.

The Ducks

There's a pair of ducks
near the road where it floods.
They are always seen,
brown feathers and beaks.

There's a pair of ducks
that nest quite happily
amongst the fronds and weeds
lining the storm drain.

There's a pair of ducks
That try every year
To raise their chicks
To survive humans and cars.

There's a pair of ducks
That survived floods
And more floods,
And then the machinery came.

There's a pair of ducks
That moved their nest
Because humans decided
The flooding was bad.

There's a pair of ducks,
Who nest where the road floods
Now, who will know,
If the ducklings survive.

There's a pair of ducks
Near the road where it floods.
They are always seen
Hopefully chicks as well.

The Window

She's sitting there
Staring out the window
At the falling dusk
Watching the clouds join
And break apart.

He's sitting there
Staring at the window
At her reflection
Watching the colours and light
Dance across her face.

She's sitting there
Staring out the window
Wondering if tomorrow
Will be a repeat of today
Or a new beginning.

He's sitting there
Staring at the window
Hoping that when the sun sets
There can be closure
But also opportunity.

They're sitting there
Staring out the window
Glancing at each other.
The night has fallen
Together, but apart

Sitting on the Train

I'm sitting on the train
Watching the trees whizz by
It doesn't look like rain
Though there's clouds in the sky

The trees are different colours
And different types as well
And under hidden arbours
Other trees also dwell

There's the silver grey of the gum tree
The wattle covered in gold
The branches, waving wild and free
Each tree bright and bold

The jacaranda purple
The multitude of brown
Variances subtle
The fan palm with its crown

The grasses with their spiky leaves
And the needles of the fir
They blow around, so much at ease
The colours sometimes blur

I'm sitting on the train
Watching the trees whizz by
And suddenly I'm home again
And the trees are waving "bye"

Summer

It's sweltering.
The sun relentlessly burns everything it touches.
Oppressive heat infiltrates the smallest space.
No cloud in sight.
No respite.

It's scorching.
The sand, soft beneath bare feet, blisters.
Scalding heat permeates everywhere.
No shade in sight.
No respite.

It's glaring.
The sea mirrors the vibrant sky.
Heat haze rises from the still water.
No end in sight.
No respite.

It's blinding.
Light reflects from every flat surface.
It floods all areas, none left with darkness.
No shadow in sight.
No respite.

The Darkness

The darkness from which I cannot hide
Is sitting there, just outside.
The shadows seep into the room
The candles do not stop the gloom.

The darkness seeps into my mind
Insidious, until defined.
It claws and creeps, and then it's here
The shadows within my mind appear.

The darkness sinks, there is no light
Shadows win against the light.
Outside is dark, inside is too,
My mind, and heart are split in two.

The darkness holds such strength and care,
It's hard to see, but always there.
The shadows sink within and find
An open heart, an open mind.

The darkness lifts, and then it's light
The sun is shining, oh, so bright.
The shadows simply fall away,
Like any other autumn day.

The darkness has gone, yet, it's there
It never, really, disappears.
But, yellow, red and orange leaves,
Are bright colours in the autumn trees.

The darkness is there, yet, it's not,
There's lightness, as well, to fill the stop.
Look beyond the shadows to see the light,
From the darkness it's always bright.

The Jacaranda

Lying underneath the jacaranda
The sun filters through the leaves,
and flowers.
I can see the kookaburra
It's laughter makes me at ease,
In my bower.

Lying underneath the jacaranda
The purple flowers float about softly
And settle.
I can see the kookaburra
It's laughter sounds oftly
Amidst the petals.

Lying underneath the jacaranda
Purple drifts down to create a carpet
Beneath me.
I can see the kookaburra
With its keen eye on a parapet
To better see.

Lying underneath the jacaranda
It's spring and flowers adorn
In vibrant colour.
I can see the Kookaburra
Laughing in the morn,
In early hour.

A New Day

The softest of colours
The barest of breeze
A new day awakens
Light filters the trees

The sun slowly rises
The birds start to sing
Animals chatter
A new day begins

The colours they brighten
Yellow, green, white, and blue

A new day continues
Its promises true

The sun blazes down
The breeze starts to blow
Clouds start to gather
The day seems to slow

The colours are sharper
Now orange and red
The day starts to quiet
The wind has now fled

The sun slowly settles
The birds are now nesting
Animals sleep
The day now is resting

The colours are gone
Only midnight remains
A new day is coming
A promise proclaimed

Summer Breeze

There's a thought within the summer breeze,
Within the trees,
it's yours, it's mine, a thought sublime
Upon the breeze.

You feel the wind upon your face,
A thought of peace.
A feeling bright, a thought that's light,
A thought of peace.

There's a thought within the summer breeze,
Within the leaves
Its mine, it's yours, no single cause
Upon the breeze.

You feel the sun upon your face,
A thought of grace.
A feeling fine, a thought divine,
A thought of grace.

There's a thought within the summer breeze,
Within the trees
It's yours, it's mine, a thought most kind
Upon the breeze.

Skimming Stones

I remember skimming stones as a child.
Finding the flattest,
The best.
The most skips,
The farthest.

I remember skimming stones as a child.
The water ripples
Getting bigger
With each skip.
Causing havoc.

I remember skimming stones as a child.
Playing with friends,
Sisters.
The best throw,
The worst.

I remember skimming stones as a child.
Season didn't matter,
Full sun
Or Dappled light.
Any weather.

I remember skimming stones as a child.
The weight of the stone,

The size,
The colour too,
Because that mattered.

I remember skimming stones as a child.
The heady days
of childhood.
Sometimes I wish
I still could.

Windy

It was windy today,
And cold,
And damp.
The clouds gathered,
Didn't join together,
The sun shone this afternoon.
It was windy today,
towels blew
On the washing line.
They were mostly dry,
Still a bit damp,
Put them into the dryer.
It was windy today,
Trees waved,
Flowers flew.
The chickens clucked
They didn't like the wind
Kept trying to escape.
It was windy today
Kids laughed
Kites flew
The branches bent
There's leaves in the trees
They waved around
It was windy today

The Sunbeam

The cat lies peacefully
Curled into a circle
Its whiskers sometimes twitch.

On the unmade bed,
Up near the pillows
A sunbeam shines, just
                                    there

The cat wakes slowly
The warmth of the sun
Filling it with indolence.

It stretches a paw
Notices the light
A sunbeam shines, just
                                    there.

The cat preens quietly
Watching the sunbeam
And the spot on the pillow.

It arches its back
Takes a few steps forward.
A sunbeam shines, just
                              there.

The cat sleeps silently
Up near the pillows
A snuffle sometimes breaks

The tail flicks about
Breaking the sunlight.
A sunbeam shines, just
                              there.

Sunrise

The light filters through the curtains
I'm already awake
It was dark the last time I looked out.

I hear the coffee machine beeping,
Letting me know,
My wakeup call is ready to drink.

With a cup in hand I open the door,
Over the horizon
The sun is just making itself known.

The sky is awash in pale oranges and pinks
To the west
It's still midnight blue.

There's a bird call, and then another
And suddenly,
The world is filled with sound.

The day is bright and fresh
Just waiting
For me to breathe again.

The Mirror

There's a mirror in my garden
not always seen.
A pond of water -
The reflection changes.

There's a mirror in my garden
sometimes grey,
sometimes blue,
sometimes branches.

There's a mirror in my garden
when there's no wind, and
no ripples
on the water.

There's a mirror in my garden,
branches, and flowers
reflecting brilliantly.
An absolute reflection.

There's a mirror in my garden.
Stare at the water,
a reflection,
no ripples.

There's a mirror in my garden.

The Mulberry Tree

There's fruit upon the mulberry tree.
The birds enjoy food that is free.
Yet underneath the branches of leaves
A secret trove is hard to see.

For underneath the branches green,
And hidden 'neath the berries gleam,
A children's fancy, can be seen
By the sun, or the moonlight sheen.

A fairy glen, a childhood dream,
Imagination runs extreme
Fairy dust, a make believe stream
Beneath the mulberry branches green.

A fort, a castle, a place of peace
A warrior, a maid, a priest.
An elven lord, a fairy niece
Whatever part, they play a piece.

For underneath the mulberry tree,
Lies a world that's make believe
Where children's dreams can achieve
Thoughts, and imagination weave.

There's fruit upon the mulberry tree.
And birds enjoy fruit that's free.
Yet underneath the branches of leaves
There's a secret world, if you believe.

The Waterhole

The ground is dry,
Rain expected for weeks,
But it hasn't come,
Yet.

The clouds gather,
The humidity so hot
That it coats every
Surface.

Instinctively they know,
The rain is coming.
Animals aware,
Alert.

The waterhole is empty
Thirsty mud waiting
For water to fill
its banks.

When the rain comes,
Creeks fill with abandon
Trees shudder
Roots stretch.

The creeks fill,
Filter to the waterhole,
Animals watch
Waiting.

The rain comes
Trickles at first,
Then a deluge
Overflows the banks.

It's quiet.
The waterhole silent
And full.
Animals slumber.

Empty

It's hot.
But I'm sitting on the pool deck
Pretending life is great,
And I'm not floundering.

Everyone
looks put together, and I guess
I'm just going with the flow,
Pretending all is good.

I know,
It's pretend, underneath
I'm paddling like a duck
Legs scrambling for purchase.

I wish,
Life could be real, and
What I show to the world
Is the real me. It's not.

Instead,
I'll laugh and smile
Say everything is fine
Until it's not.

It's hot,
But I'm sitting on the pool deck
Thinking that water looks cold
And empty.

Twilight

I'm waiting
I know it's coming
The anticipation makes it harder.

Every email is met
With anguish,
Then joy, then sadness.

I look at gifts given,
Throughout the years,
And remember happier times.

They're here,
Yet they're not.
Only their body remains present.

Their mind no longer recognising
Family, or loved ones.
Eyes glazed in confusion

If I had a choice
They'd live forever
In their prime, engaged with life.

Instead they're in their twilight
Days pass
And memories fade.
It's hard to say goodbye.

Eternal

The ground is filled
The atmosphere electric
Spectators young and old
Flags and banners

Gone are the days
of the Gabba Hill
When drunk spectators
Heckled the opposition

When there was just
The cheering of the crowd
Or the jeering
When a catch was dropped

Gone are the days
When all you could hear
Was hundreds of radios
All playing the commentary

When the players would talk
In between balls,
And sign bats and hats
For excited kids.

Now all you can hear
Is music and fireworks
All you can see
Are security guards and screens.

The grounds have changed
As have the players.
But the game stays the same,
Eternal.

Saturday Afternoon

It's a Saturday afternoon, and
Quite breezy at the beach.
There's a marquee up,
Tables and chairs as well.

We're all dressed up, in
Costumes subtle and bold.
Things beginning with A -
Angel, alchemist, athlete.

Kids run around, playing
There are kayaks and paddle boards
Footballs and balloons
Games and music.

Who can climb the highest
In the trees.
A bobbing apple relay -
Girls versus boys. Girls win.

A birthday cake, and
A unicorn pinata, with
A blindfold and a stick.
Way too many lollies!

There's chatter and laughter, and
Children full of joy,
Hyper with too much sugar,
Or silent in exhaustion.

The sun starts to set,
Bags are packed.
It's a Saturday afternoon, and
Quite breezy at the beach.

9 789357 690188